# The Ultimate Board Member's Book

A 1-Hour Guide
to Understanding and Fulfilling
Your Role and Responsibilites

# Companion Books

## Fund Raising Realities
## Every Board Member Must Face

A 1-Hour Crash Course on Raising
Major Gifts for Nonprofit Organizations

*David Lansdowne*

If every board member of every non-profit organization across America read this book, it's no exaggeration to say that millions upon millions of additional dollars would be raised.

How could it be otherwise when, after spending just *one* hour with this gem, board members everywhere would understand virtually everything they need to know about raising major gifts.

David Lansdowne distills the essence of major gifts fundraising, puts it in the context of 47 "realities," and delivers it all in unfailingly clear prose.

Among the *Top Three* bestselling fundraising books of all time.

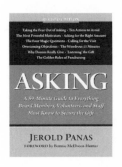

## ASKING

A 59-Minute Guide to Everything
Board Members, Volunteers, and Staff
Must Know to Secure the Gift

*Jerold Panas*

It ranks right up there with public speaking. Nearly all of us fear it. And yet it's critical to the success of our organizations. Asking for money. It makes even the stout-hearted quiver.

But now comes a book, *Asking,* and short of a medical elixir, it's the next best thing for emboldening board members, volunteers, and staff to ask with skill, finesse … and powerful results.

What *Asking* convincingly shows is that it doesn't take stellar sales skills to be an effective asker. Nearly everyone, regardless of their persuasive ability, can become an effective fundraiser if they follow Panas' step-by-step guidelines.

### Emerson & Church, Publishers
www.emersonandchurch.com

# THE
# ULTIMATE
## BOARD MEMBER'S BOOK

A 1-Hour Guide
To Understanding and Fulfilling
Your Role and Responsibilites

## KAY SPRINKEL GRACE

Emerson
& Church
PUBLISHERS

*First printed January 2009*

*10 9 8 7 6 5 4 3*

*Printed in the United States of America*

*This text is printed on acid-free paper.*

---

*Copies of this book are available from the publisher at discount when purchased in quantity for boards of directors or staff.*

---

*Emerson & Church, Publishers*
*28A Park Street • Medfield, MA 02052*
*Tel. 508-359-0019 • Fax 508-359-2703*
*www.emersonandchurch.com*

**Library of Congress Cataloging-in-Publication Data**

Grace, Kay Sprinkel.
  The ultimate board member's book : a 1-hour guide to understanding and fulfilling your role and responsibilities / Kay Sprinkel Grace. — Rev. ed.
      p. cm.
  Includes index.
  ISBN 978-1-889102-39-9 (pbk. : alk. paper)
  1. Nonprofit organizations. 2. Leadership. 3. Voluntarism.
I. Title.
  HD62.6.G714 2009
  658.4'22—dc22
                                    2008034691

# FOREWORD

I'm not a theorist, I'm a doer. So when I think about the nonprofit sector and my service within it, I think in practical terms and about what works. And as you're about to learn, *The Ultimate Board Member's Book* works. It is focused, practical, and exceptionally readable.

I've served on a variety of nonprofit boards, large and small. I have chaired them, cheered them, challenged them, and in some cases even changed them. As a result, I know firsthand the importance of having a high performing board and have used this book many times to guide me.

Not that building an "ultimate" board is easy. Not by a stretch. But there's a tremendous payoff for making the effort ... and I mean that literally. Recently, a U.S. Trust study found that among high net worth donors – those with $5 million or more in assets – one of the top four determinants of where they contribute money is respect for the organization's leadership.

In my experience, high performing boards have certain core attributes, as Grace underscores. Among them are: understanding boundaries; respecting each other and staff; mastering the mission; communicating the vision; and living the values. When these givens are in place, there is stability and the opportunity for growth and impact. Work gets done.

*The Ultimate Board Member's Book* advances the idea that board service is "noble." To that I would add inspiriting, uplifting, transcendent even. After a 30-year career in magazine publishing, I now get as much, if not more, satisfaction from my service to the Corporation for Public Broadcasting, to College Track, and to Higher Ground, all worthy endeavors with sterling boards.

To these organizations I try to bring the same analytical rigor and emphasis on effective results that I brought to my business pursuits. I wake up every morning brimming with ideas to help these life-enhancing organizations become better still. I wish the same for everyone who reads this instructive and illuminating book.

*Portola Valley, Calif.*                                    Chris Boskin

*Chris Boskin, Chair of the Board for the Corporation for Public Broadcasting, is a respected veteran of magazine publishing, with a career that has included publishing and marketing positions with Worth Media, the New Yorker magazine, Hearst Corporation, East West Network, and Knapp Communications. She is currently a consultant to several media companies.*

# INTRODUCTION

The call has come. You've been asked to serve on a nonprofit board. You have mixed feelings.

If you're new to boards, you may be anxious about your responsibilities and what's expected of you, while feeling pride and a certain sense of accomplishment that you've been selected.

If you're an experienced board member, willing to be called into service again, you may have feelings of renewed pride, or even joy, and may be thinking, "This is the board I've been waiting to serve on!"

Whatever your motivation for joining a board, and whatever your inner voices are saying, this book is for you. It is drawn from observation of literally thousands of board members and hundreds of boards over my long and satisfying career as a consultant to nonprofit organizations and also from my own experiences as a board member.

If it is occasionally light-hearted, that doesn't diminish the importance of your work – it merely says that board service, like all of life, is a serious business that needn't always be taken so seriously.

Enjoy – and you have my fervent hope that *The Ultimate Board Member's Book* will help you be what others will describe as ... the ultimate board member!

*San Francisco, Calif.*                    Kay Sprinkel Grace

# CONTENTS

### III • How Boards Work

### IV • Meetings

### V • Development and Fundraising

# NOBLE SERVICE

# 1

# America's Nonprofit Sector

The governance of an organization that serves community needs (whether locally, nationally, or globally) has been placed in your hands.

The wisdom you show, the decisions you make, your willingness to give time and money, and to serve thoughtfully throughout your term have implications far beyond a board meeting, or even your board service. The decisions and actions you take now will have value and impact for years to come.

When you join a board, you join a legion of men and women across the U.S. and around the world who willingly give their "time, talent, and treasure" to advance organizations that embody their vision and values.

America's nonprofit sector, of which you're a proud part, is unique. Its impact is felt in communities everywhere, from Los Angeles to New York, from Fond du Lac to Tuscaloosa, from Prague to Singapore.

In fact, our nation's commitment to philanthropy is one of its most distinguishing features and among our finest social exports.

All of which means you're part of a prodigious force of capable individuals – once unique to America but now growing around the world – who realize they can be part of something bigger than themselves.

Being a board member in America's nonprofit sector is one of the most enriching experiences you'll ever have. It will be frustrating at times, and exhilarating at others; it will make demands, but give huge rewards; it will connect you with people who will add new dimensions to your life.

And, when your experience is over, you should be assured that not only is there hope for the future, but you yourself have helped make that hope possible.

# 2

# Your Unique Role

More than one nonprofit CEO, having had a bad day – or year – with a board, will seriously question why he needs to have a board. It's no wonder.

Decisions would certainly be faster if he didn't have to wait for meetings and consensus. Troubling issues could be handled more directly if there weren't personnel or development committees to consult. And, the CEO could always hire a larger fundraising staff to raise money.

So, why do we have boards? In reality, for checks and balances.

Because nonprofits exist to meet the needs of the community, and since these organizations work a great deal with other people's money (such as gifts and grants), the law requires that community members be present to hold the organization "in trust," to help ensure that community needs are represented and that funds are spent wisely.

Further, because a nonprofit's financial resources are limited, staff must be kept at a reasonable size. Board members, by serving as ambassadors and advocates in the community, augment the organization's resources and enhance its impact.

All of which makes your role unique. On the one hand, you hold the organization in trust and are legally and financially responsible for its well-being. On the other hand, while it's not your job to manage daily operations, it is your responsibility to ensure that the person in charge manages all human and financial resources of the organization effectively, appropriately, and honestly.

And these are just the formal responsibilities – the tip of the iceberg, as you will discover.

# 3

# Why You Were Recruited

Increasingly, board members are recruited according to a matrix. The existing board is analyzed to determine the areas where it needs to be strengthened.

These criteria are drawn from the institutional plan, with the goal of building a board whose qualities will best support the organization's vision and goals.

This process can affect the role you're expected to play. If, for example, you're a marketing whiz, don't be surprised if you're asked to chair the marketing committee and its planning process. If you successfully guided another organization through a multi-million dollar capital campaign, you'll likely find yourself heading a development committee that's planning a major gifts push.

If whoever recruited you didn't clarify why you were

selected, now is the time to ask.

Now is also the time to communicate your own personal or professional reasons for joining the board.

Are you there to learn a new skill (such as fundraising) or to bring an existing skill to bear for the benefit of the organization?

Do you represent a professional sector linked to the organization (such as a psychologist serving on a mental health board) and therefore see yourself in more of a professional advisory role?

Or are you what is lovingly known as a "community volunteer" – that fading phenomenon of socially conscious people who find themselves bringing their passion, intellect, and connections to a wide variety of boards?

Be clear about your own desires – they are critical to sustaining your motivation.

# 4

# What the Job Entails

It's hard to be the ultimate board member if you don't know what's expected of you.

Whether you were enlisted with a formal contract or simply a handshake, there's no escaping the fact that by joining a board you're signing on for a whole set of responsibilities.

At any given time, expect also to be called upon to be ambassador, compliance officer, policy-maker, fundraiser, advocate, or manager.

Whatever the specifics of your situation, understand that good board members:

• Attend board and committee meetings.

• Read and understand materials and publications sent in advance of meetings.

• Treat all information discussed or exchanged in confidence.

• Ensure that appropriate financial, legal, tax, and personnel review systems are in place.

• Understand financial information and processes.

• Review and follow policies previously set and cause new policies to be created if needed.

• Respect staff and their time, and know the boundaries between board and staff jobs.

Perhaps most important, good board members are diligent. About everything. Finances, CEO evaluations, fundraising – you name it. They ask tough questions and expect honest answers.

# 5

# The Time Commitment

Some organizations seem unable or unwilling to correctly assess the time they expect from board members. They end up conveying unrealistic expectations – usually downplaying the time commitment. This can be a great source of friction in the relationship between the CEO and board.

Whether you're a new recruit to the board or a standing member asked to serve on a subcommittee, ask the organization to be absolutely clear about the time commitment. How many meetings? How many committees? How much work outside of board meetings and committees? How many hours spent in fundraising training, cultivation sessions, special events?

Withhold your decision until you know exactly what's expected.

Down the line, if you're unable to fulfill the time commitment you made, it's important to relay that information to those who are counting on you.

If the change is permanent – you have a new job, baby, travel schedule – ask for reassignment or a leave from the board. If the change is temporary (an unexpected trip, health issue or parent duty), simply work out a schedule that allows you to resume your duties when the time is better.

One of the gifts we give as board members is our time. Although we cannot hold it or capture it, it is a hard commodity. If it is wasted by others, we become resentful.

Be respectful of time – yours and others – and give it as generously as you can to the boards on which you serve.

# 6

# Deriving Satisfaction From Your Service

Board service is a form of philanthropy – it is the voluntary giving of your time and talents (and "treasure" of course!) to an organization whose mission you endorse and whose values you share.

Whereas your designation as a "good" board member depends on a range of objective criteria; being a *satisfied* board member is how *you* feel about what you're doing.

Three key factors will determine the satisfaction you derive from board service:

• How much you believe in the issues the organization is addressing.

• How well your values match those espoused by the organization.

• How motivating you find the tasks to which you're assigned.

If your passion is mental health or education or the environment, you'll derive the most satisfaction from organizations addressing these issues. While other agencies may intrigue you, or perhaps seem appropriate for your own professional or personal ambitions, chances are your greatest satisfaction will come from serving organizations that tackle the issues you're most passionate about.

Secondly, it is important that the things you value – be they equal access to education, freedom of worship, dignity for the aging – are evident in the organization's mission and consistently displayed.

Finally, if you're to be a satisfied board member, you'll need to plumb your own motivations and work with the organization to structure assignments that keep you energized.

If you're a high achiever, for example, you'll want to be recognized for what you do. There's nothing wrong with that. Ask for and accept assignments that provide you with opportunities to excel and be recognized.

If, instead, you enjoy board service for the pleasure of being affiliated with others who share your interests, you'll want to serve on events or other committees so you can work collaboratively with others.

Remember, the list of board member responsibilities defines what the organization needs from you; your own passions and motivations define what you need from the organization.

# 7

# Honoring Your Position

It is a special privilege to be a board member, but some abuse the privilege. The ways are many – some more subtle than others.

Overtly, we see the abuse with high profile arts organizations where board members insist on admission, seating, and access privileges that may not be part of the board member agreement.

Less obvious to the public, but more distressing to the organization, is the internal abuse of power that occurs when board members attempt to micromanage the organization. There is a distinct line between responsible behavior and inappropriate interference.

If you're on the finance committee and see expenditures way out of balance with revenue, it *is* your job to share your concerns with the board chair.

It is inappropriate, and an abuse of power, to march into the headquarters of the organization and demand to see receipts, checks, payables, and receivables unless and until the CEO invites you to lend your expertise in the area of financial management.

Still another common abuse of power is best described by a phrase drawn from football: an "end run." Going around the CEO, directly to a staff person, can be demoralizing not only to the CEO, but to the organization as well. It puts the staff person in a compromised position and can bifurcate the agency.

Honor your role as a board member by respecting the responsibilities of staff members, and the lines that separate you. Additionally, don't ask for more than you're willing to work for, or pay for.

You erode your power and position by abusing it.

# HOLDING IN TRUST

# 8

# The Mission of Your Organization

As a board member, a large part of your responsibility is to be a "keeper of the mission." Given that challenge, you need to understand the concept of mission, and what the mission of your organization is.

Mission is *why* your organization exists. It centers around the human or societal need your group is addressing. For March of Dimes, for instance, the mission is "to improve the health of babies by preventing birth defects, premature birth, and infant mortality."

As a board member, it's imperative to comprehend the mission and insist on a strong mission statement. It is the message you carry into the community. It guides, inspires, energizes, and describes the importance of what you're doing to those you're recruiting for the board, soliciting for gifts, or involving as volunteers.

While brevity isn't required, some of the best mission statements are summarized in a single tagline or phrase. The American Red Cross's "Help can't wait" comes to mind.

As a board member, your ability to "keep" the mission is directly linked to your ability to articulate it. And that requires regular exposure and vigilance.

One sure way is to keep the focus on *why* you do what you do, not just on *what* you do. Site tours and meetings with people who have benefited from your organization can keep you reminded of why you got involved in the first place.

Secondly, an annual "Mission Immersion" day – one in which every board member spends five or six hours meeting people and visiting programs – is very powerful for reconnecting board members with the mission.

Thirdly, board meetings should always include a "mission moment" – five to ten minutes in the middle of the meeting to hear from a grateful patient, happy teacher, transformed client, satisfied parent, or other individual who shares their pleasure with what you've done for them and for others.

A fourth way is to ensure good rotation on your board. This can keep your group infused with people whose wonder and curiosity will offset any decline of energy among those who have served for a long time.

Finally, you keep the mission fresh by looking out the windows, not gazing into mirrors. The mission must always be grounded in the why, and the why is as current as a refreshed Google page.

# 9

# Championing
# the Values

In addition to being a keeper of the mission, you have to be a champion and guardian of the organization's values – those deeply held beliefs that guide its decisions, programs, and marketing.

The late John W. Gardner, in his book *On Leadership*, listed "Affirming values" as the second among his nine tasks of leaders. He was right.

Because nonprofits are driven by values, and because development (including fundraising, which we'll discuss later) is the process of identifying shared values with people, it's important that you know, understand, and support the organization's values.

There are several dimensions to your job here. One is your own commitment. If the organization supports issues which are out of synch with your values, then you shouldn't be involved unless you think you can change the direction.

Another is your responsibility to ensure that the organization's marketing and development materials – electronic, printed or visual – clearly convey its values. After all, an organization's values are what ultimately draws people to it.

A third is your responsibility to articulate the values. Whether in formal presentations such as speakers' bureaus and meeting reports or informal conversations with people, be sure to convey not only what the organization does and why, but how the work underscores its values. How, for example, an adult day program keeps people independent and respects their dignity. How a school committed to diversity embraces a cross-section of its community in programming *and* hiring.

People sometimes get values and mission confused. They are different, but both are part of the why that motivates people to start organizations and get others involved.

# 10

# Your Legal Responsibilities

Each state in the U.S. has defined the legal responsibilities and liabilities for nonprofit organizations and their board members.

Your job as a board member is to ask for this information, know what the laws are, ensure that you're operating within them, and know when as a board member your organization is putting your legal responsibilities to the test.

Understand, if as a result of your organization's activities someone is injured, killed, or wrongly dealt with, and if that person sues, you are liable. There is insurance for officers and directors; insist that your organization have it.

But beyond that you have a responsibility to your community. You are called a trustee for good reason:

you hold the organization in trust.

You should also be familiar with the by-laws and articles of incorporation, as these provide the legal and operational framework for your organization. By-laws outline the structure, rules, and protocols for your organization. Articles of Incorporation define why you exist and how you propose to operate.

As a board member, it's your responsibility to ensure that your organization is in compliance with them.

Few people take the time to read these documents. To be sure, they aren't page-turners. Still, it's good to be acquainted with your by-laws. Some time, at some meeting, you may need to know what they say to resolve an issue or make a prudent decision.

# 11

# The Right To Be Informed

This is an incontestable duty and right.

Because you hold the legal and fiduciary responsibility for the organization, you must know the truth about all facets of its operations. In bureaucratic or just plain weary organizations, this information is sometimes withheld from the board by staff or, in some cases, by board leadership from the rest of the board.

Transparency, with its dimensions of full accountability and disclosure, is the watchword of 21st century philanthropy. Donors want it, board members should demand it, and the community deserves it.

To prevent any withholding of information, make sure there's sufficient board involvement in financial, legal, and programmatic evaluation. And, at the first sign that information is incomplete or guarded, ask questions.

Then keep asking until you're persuaded that either you're on to something or that your suspicions are unfounded.

As a board member, even if figures aren't your forte, learn to read a financial statement and balance sheet so you can ask intelligent questions. Furthermore, insist that all internal and external evaluations – even negative ones – be communicated to the board.

Granted, there will be instances when it's inappropriate for the full board to know all the details of a situation. Sensitive personnel issues come to mind, in which individuals or their families would suffer personal damage if information were circulated. These situations are best kept in the executive committee.

But, excepting these few instances, exercise your right as the "owner" of the organization to be completely in the know.

# 12

# Conflicts of Interest

Does a printer who serves on a board and offers a deep discount for handling the organization's holiday mailing have a conflict of interest? No.

Does a financial advisor, who makes a commission from investment transactions, have a conflict of interest when asked by his fellow board members for an objective appraisal of the endowment's management? Yes.

While there's plenty of gray area in most conflict of interest situations, some are so obvious, such as the latter, that little discussion is required. In the first case, if the printer's quote is competitive, no real conflict exists.

There are other conflict of interest issues that surface on some boards. Here are a few examples:

• Board members who are parents of children attending an independent school may find themselves having to make difficult decisions affecting their children.

• Performing artists invited to sit on the boards of organizations at which they perform may also find themselves in conflict.

• Organizations whose by-laws require client representation may find that those clients have difficulty making tough choices regarding programs in which they've been involved.

As a board member, don't put yourself into a situation where there's a potential conflict. Make your difficulty known and absent yourself from discussions in which the conflict could influence your decision making.

On many boards, there's a benign tolerance of mild conflicts of interest. It grows out of affection and respect for the individuals involved, a tendency to look the other way, an unwillingness to rock the boat, or raise an unpleasant issue.

If this is the case with your board, make it a policy with the recruitment of new board members that apparent conflicts of interests need to be addressed and managed. Better yet, if the potential conflict is so obvious, don't recruit that person.

Remember, you have a "duty of loyalty" to not put your personal interests ahead of those of the organization.

# HOW BOARDS WORK

# 13

# Qualities of an Effective Board

Defining board effectiveness is a challenge, but there is a simple truth to guide the inquiry: *boards that work, work.*

The board of an established independent school with abundant prestige and alumni has a notably different focus than the board of a start-up agency serving meals to shut-in seniors.

These two boards will also have different composition, and different operating cultures. And yet, some standards for effectiveness are applicable to these and all boards:

1) There is a shared vision for the organization and the impact it will have if the vision is fulfilled.

2) The shared values of the board members and the

organization are understood and frame the goals.

3) The mission is clear and revisited often: it is understood and shared by the board with the community.

4) Goals and strategies are defined and endorsed.

5) Board assignments are clear, specific, reasonable, and matched to the board member's motivation.

6) Board members support the organization financially as well as with their time.

7) Board meetings are guided by an agenda, tolerant of diverse opinions, and dedicated to reaching agreements in keeping with the organization's mission.

8) There's a sense of teamwork when approaching a major challenge and shared satisfaction when the challenge is met.

9) Board recruitment is systematic and based on identifying people who are needed to achieve the vision and goals.

10) Board member rotation is encouraged, but turnover from dissatisfaction is minimal.

11) Board self-evaluation is conducted annually and the results used to improve board knowledge and performance.

That's a pretty tall order. How does your board measure up?

# 14

# Decision Making

One size doesn't fit all when it comes to describing how boards make decisions. Generally speaking, boards operate on the consensus model, which is both the strength and the weakness of nonprofit governance.

Because boards represent the community and its various constituencies, the value of having broad input and agreement on key issues is unquestioned. With well-facilitated discussions, people feel heard and share in the decisions. This is especially important as it leads to greater willingness to raise money, be advocates, roll up one's sleeves, and get involved.

If that is the strength of the consensus model, the weakness is the time it consumes. Corporate executives, accoustomed to swift decisions with little consensus, may chafe at the pace and detail that characterize nonprofit decision-making.

Others, who perhaps have the experience or the

knowledge to know what should be done, are impatient with those who need to be educated before they can make the decision.

As a board member, be a catalyst in helping your board make decisions that couple both wisdom and efficiency.

• Be sure that meetings have an agenda and that those who wish to participate have a chance to do so.

• Respect diversity of opinion and style in decision-making. When a decision is made, see that it's not overturned by an executive committee without board input.

• Stand up for your dissenting point; don't succumb to group-think before advocating for your position.

• When choosing leaders, make sure they're capable of running meetings and are skilled at building consensus.

• Determine what decisions can be made by staff, and respect their judgment.

And, finally, be a participant. Give and take. Mix it up. More than anything, that'll help your board arrive at the right decisions.

# 15

# The Board
# and Planning

To effectively recruit board members, raise money, market your organization, or conduct any kind of programming, there has to be a comprehensive institutional plan that is strategic, inclusive, and realistic.

It must be based on the organization's vision, but framed by the realities of the human and financial resources available, and the social and economic climate in which you're operating.

Gone are the days when nonprofits could blithely operate without a strategy or even a published budget. Today, those on whom your organization depends for funding expect you to have a detailed blueprint.

What is the board member's role in this process?

Your first role is to ask if there is a plan. If there isn't, find out what it will take to get the process started.

Your second job is to insist on board member involvement in the process. Even though much of the plan is program related and carried out by staff, there are parts of it (board development and fund development, for example) that land squarely in your job description.

Furthermore, you cannot recruit and retain a board or cultivate and engage donors if you don't understand the plan and feel a part of the decisions that shaped it.

Lastly, ask that a team of board members be appointed to work with staff in a process that will result not only in a workable plan, but also in a system for monitoring its implementation.

# 16

# Collective Wisdom, Individual Initiative

Although you have considerable responsibilities as an individual board member, you have the duty as well to ensure that your board acts effectively as a whole.

When a decision is made by a board, even with dissenting votes, it is the decision of the group. Your job is to ensure its implementation.

Not that you'll always be comfortable doing so. There are times when you'll contest the wording, the timing, or the strategy. But after voicing your dissent, line up with the rest of the team.

Of course, if a decision or action challenges your basic values, that's a different story altogether. Then, you may need to rethink your involvement with the organization and the board.

The importance of your role as an individual will be

strengthened by your participation as part of the group. Your opinions and ideas will gain further respect when people see that you're able to submerge disappointment in favor of working collaboratively with the board and maintaining the integrity of its decisions.

And, if and when you realize that a decision with which you disagreed turned out to be a good decision after all, let the others know. Your voice will gain stature.

# 17

# Committees and Task Forces

As a board member, you'll be expected to serve on one or more committees or task forces. How can you make the experience more productive?

First, ask for a goal statement for your committee. What are the objectives? What is the purpose? What outcomes are sought? Who is the staff support, and what can you expect in terms of assistance?

And, if you've been asked to chair the committee, ask for a job description. Find out how much time you'll need to spend, and what the other expectations are.

Second, have an agenda for every meeting. If there's no purpose to the meeting, don't have it.

Third, make sure all members of the committee know the larger goals and outcomes so there's a heightened sense of the importance of what they're doing. If people understand the why, they'll more readily get going with the task.

Fourth, be sure you're prepared to support the recommendations of your committee at the full board meeting. You may be called upon to answer a question or provide background on one or more of them.

•••

As a board member, you can influence the effectiveness of committee meetings and the quality of the recommendations and decisions made. The key is to be attentive, speak out when needed, ask for measurable outcomes, promote teamwork, and, yes, have some fun all the while.

# 18

# Working with Other Volunteers

Often as a board member you'll interact with a range of volunteers in the organization. These individuals serve in many capacities:

• Auxiliary members, for example, often give hundreds of hours each year to work in thrift shops, gift stores, hospital rooms, or on fundraising events. They can become alienated from the "big board" if they're not respected or appropriately recognized. As a board member, if you observe this happening, take action. Ask for a more formal recognition program for outstanding non-board volunteers.

• Program volunteers are those in the classrooms, physical therapy rooms, pediatric wards, or other places where it's appropriate and helpful to have trained volunteers. As a board member, ask to meet some of these volunteers as part of your efforts to connect more closely with the mission.

• Lastly, there are other kinds of volunteers who offer professional services on a pro-bono basis. These can include the broker who handles stock gifts without commission (or turns his commission back to the organization), the accountant who does the books for a small organization, or the non-board lawyer who troubleshoots a difficult personnel situation.

Some of these individuals, seeking more involvement, may be candidates for board committees. Having non-board members on certain committees stretches the human resources and provides opportunities for new talent to emerge.

As a board member, your interaction with any of these non-board volunteers should be one of professionalism, gratitude, and recognition for the time they give.

# 19

# Developing Yourself As a Board Member

Each board is different. That means you have an opportunity with each organization to evolve further, or in different ways, as a board member.

You were recruited for what you'd bring to the board – expertise, connections, representation from new constituencies, previous experience – but part of being the ultimate board member is to use these reasons as a starting point for building your board service. What you can become is up to you.

I hope you're already gleaning some ways to develop yourself as a board member by reading this book. Here are a few others that come to mind:

• At your own board meetings insist not only on "mission moments," but request occasional presentations by experts in governance, planning, endowment management, and financial reporting for nonprofits.

• Keep yourself invigorated by getting close to the program, by learning the stories, and being able to describe the impact of your organization. Look for opportunities to tell these stories at churches, service clubs, and other organizations as well as at the gym, on the golf course or at work.

• Within your own community, connect with board members of other organizations and look for collaborative opportunities for boards to come together and discuss community, not just organizational, issues.

Increased knowledge about the organization, and confidence in your role as a board member, will enhance your ability to be an advocate. In turn, this advocacy will increase your pride and help you become the passionate pragmatist your organization wants you to be.

It will also keep you enthusiastic about your service not only to this board, but for the next.

# 20

# Subverting Mediocrity

Every day, increasing numbers of corporate executives, marketing gurus, physicians, lawyers, accountants, and bankers gather in nonprofit boardrooms.

Their combined expertise, which is formidable, should move the entire sector forward more thoughtfully and energetically than any other. And yet, with alarming frequency, this fails to happen.

It's as if capable decision-makers and nimble thinkers endure a process upon entering the nonprofit boardroom that reduces, if not nullifies, their leadership drive and determination.

There is a slide to mediocrity and an observable lowering of expectations and performance. Individuals who regularly make decisions involving millions of dollars find themselves squabbling over the expenditure of

$2,500 to replace an antiquated computer. Or quibbling over the director's salary (which often is considerably lower than what board members are paid in their own professions).

As a board member, you have a responsibility to subvert mediocrity. Just as you shouldn't stand by silently when the organization's management is faltering, neither should you allow the board's leadership to deteriorate.

When you see your fellow board members forgetting their leadership skills and their capacity to envision and act, speak up: "I think that's something for staff to address – I'd like us to focus on more substantive issues." Or, "I see that's a concern to many, but I don't think this is the right forum to discuss it. Perhaps the Chair would agree to have two or three of us work with staff to address it."

The nonprofit sector deserves the very best leadership possible. As a board member, it's your mandate not only to lead and govern, but to ensure that others do as well.

# MEETINGS

# 21

# The Purpose of Board Meetings

The purpose of board meetings is twofold.

On the one hand, and as you would expect, you attend to review financial reports, discuss new policy recommendations, hear the CEO's report of recent activities, and act upon committee recommendations.

But those agenda items are also the framework for something equally important: the creative interaction of the board itself.

Board meetings that fulfill their true purpose do the following:

- Promote a sense of teamwork.
- Reinforce the shared vision.
- Afford time to recount stories and successes.
- Connect board members with the work of staff.
- Offer stimulation for ideas.

• Provide opportunities for social interaction, and,

• Reinforce the overall sense of the mission and its importance in the community.

That's a big assignment. But if you've ever attended such a meeting, you know the feeling of exhilaration. The air practically crackles.

Unfortunately, you're probably all too familiar with a different scenario – board meetings characterized by dissent, domination by a few, and general disorganization.

While even these meetings may eventually cover the agenda items, the other key component, bonding as a group, will be missing. Without that sense of group commitment, individual commitments often falter.

As a part of the board you have an immense opportunity to make a difference in the quality of its meetings and its deliberations. Whether your gatherings soar or merely hover, make sure you're getting the most out of the meetings by putting the most into the meetings.

Be prepared, be focused, be there. And being there doesn't simply mean occupying a chair. Turn off your cell phone. Park thoughts of work outside with your car. Ask questions, participate in discussions, help smooth dissent, and be a problem solver.

# 22

# Attendance Required

Generally speaking, if you're to be a productive member you have to attend board meetings.

One key reason is to ensure a quorum. Otherwise, the board can't take formal action and may as well adjourn. Everyone's time will have been wasted, and decisions will be delayed until the next meeting. But there are other important reasons you should attend.

First, if you're not present, you can't fulfill your responsibility as it relates to decision-making, policy creation, financial approval, and other key transactions that take place at meetings.

Second, being on a board is an opportunity to develop new relationships and a spirit of camaraderie. Even if this isn't important to you, it is to others. They want to know you.

Third, to stay informed about the organization and have a dynamic sense of its accomplishments to convey to others, you need to hear about those achievements firsthand. And, the best place to hear this is at board meetings.

To be sure, there will be occasions when you cannot attend board meetings. But if your absence becomes the norm, you'll be resented for taking a seat from someone who could be a more productive participant.

# 23

# Your Responsibility After Meetings

While being a productive and thoughtful participant at board meetings is important, too many board members feel that their responsibilities end when the meeting is adjourned.

If you want to exercise your leadership and advance the organization, you'll have to work between board meetings. Here's some of the work you'll be expected to do:

• If you're on a committee, you'll usually have quarterly or more frequent meetings. Increasingly, the "work" of the board takes place at the committee level and is endorsed at board meetings.

• If you're involved in development and fundraising, you'll absolutely need to work between board meetings to complete your assignments, participate in cultivation events, and make solicitation calls.

• If you're assigned to the financial side of board work, you'll find yourself meeting with investment managers, bankers, endowment specialists, and others (and often that's in addition to finance committee meetings).

• If planning is your expertise, look forward to an annual expenditure of time to evaluate and refresh the strategic plan. You'll also need to periodically check on the plan's progress for reports at board meetings.

• If programs are your passion, you'll likely find yourself spending time between board meetings talking with program staff, visiting sites, and meeting with community people linked to your mission.

In short, the more you work on behalf of the board, the better the board will work.

# 24

# Bored or Board: It's Up to You

Board meetings tend to fall in the category of things people complain about but do little to improve. It's like the little boy who grouses at school every day about the peanut butter sandwich in his lunch box. Finally, a friend says, "Why don't you ask your mom to make a different sandwich?" The little boy replies, "My mom? I make my lunch myself!"

In large measure, the quality and spirit of board meetings is up to you. What you ask for in terms of content and quality, how you participate and prepare, and the way in which you follow up on decisions all affect the productivity and enjoyment of board meetings.

Here are some key points to keep in mind.

• Come prepared. When you're mailed a board packet, read it beforehand, rather than page through the material minutes before the meeting.

- Come on time and stay through the whole meeting. Staggered attendance is disruptive to board decision-making. It isn't a good idea to have a "rolling quorum," though some board meetings seem to operate on that basis.

- Expect an agenda, and expect it to be followed. If it isn't, ask why.

- If discussions drag on or become contentious without resolution, call the question.

- If you can't change the tempo or tenor of the meeting, work with leadership before the next meeting to improve the situation.

One good way to reduce the "bored" aspect of meetings is to work towards an issues, rather than "show and tell," focus.

Said another way, rather than listening to report after report (which you could easily read at home anyway), emphasize "big picture" discussions, those centering on the internal and external influences facing your organization. The change of pace is energizing.

Finally, remember the "mission moment" – something presented at the meeting that will excite you, inspire you, and leave you with a story to tell when you're in your ambassadorial or fundraising role.

# 25

# Regional and National Meetings

Sitting in board meetings month after month, and hearing the challenges faced in funding, ticket sales, medical repayments, homeless issues, adolescent mental health, it is easy to get cranky, critical – or, on the other end of the telescope – to lose sight of the big picture.

If your organization is part of a regional or national association that welcomes board members at its annual conferences or meetings, ask to go. If possible, take a few days from your usual work (or retirement activities) and sign up.

Those who attend meetings of Alliance for Children & Families, Dance/USA, League of American Orchestras, American Museum Association or other networks of cultural, arts, health, environmental, social or other service providers come away with renewed respect for their own organization, an enhanced sense of not being alone in the universe and, very often, a greater appreciation for their own CEO or development officer.

Board member renewal is more than just signing on for another board term. It is the constant awareness of the importance of your role, the many variables that affect that role and your ability to do well at it.

Stepping out into a larger world of which your organization is a part gives you a broader view not only of your organization, but of its importance and the potential role you can play.

# DEVELOPMENT AND FUNDRAISING

# 26

# Investment, Not Obligation

Much of today's giving – from board members (where giving has to start) to those in the community who respond to your appeals – is increasingly done from a sense of wanting to invest in community programs that are making a difference. Seldom are large gifts given or renewed out of a sense of obligation.

Nearly two decades ago, Peter Drucker commented in *The Wall Street Journal* that "people no longer give to charity, they buy into results." He was prophetic as always.

Increasingly, people invest in success. They look for impact. They identify with issues and, in many cases, shop for the organizations that are effectively addressing those issues. The words "contribution" and "donation" are relatively passive, but "investment" is dynamic.

As a board member, when you talk with people about making an investment, stress that it's not just in the organization you represent, it's in the community. They are giving as much *through* you as *to* you. That idea alone is new and invigorating to many donors.

And the return on investment is obvious. It is inspiring to the donor that his values are being acted on by the organization as it delivers programming and services that have a community impact.

Understand this repositioning of both the way to ask and the impact of the gift. You can put away the tin cup. You no longer need to feel as though you're begging for money for a needy organization.

Instead, talk with people about how their investment, channelled through your organization, is meeting prescribed needs in the community and is having a genuine impact on changing and saving lives.

# 27

# Philanthropy, Development, And Fundraising

Philanthropy has several dimensions and is perhaps best defined as all voluntary action for the public good. As a board member, you are engaged in philanthropy.

It encompasses everything you do – giving, asking, joining, and serving – to advance programs that, in the words of Robert Payton, first Director of the Center on Philanthropy at Indiana University, "ease human suffering or enhance human potential."

Distinguished from philanthropy is *development*, or relationship building. Development uncovers shared values between people and organizations.

It does so accidentally, as when you talk with someone and discover what they care about. But development can also be deliberate, as when the organization's staff identify and research likely donors – or when donors with an interest in your issue identify, research, and connect with you.

Finally, there's *fundraising*. It comes last, because it's easiest when you've uncovered the shared values of others – people who think and dream as you do and want to join with you in meeting compelling community needs.

As much as you may shudder when you think of asking someone for money, if you look upon it as the end result of a process that's inviting, supportive, and revealing of values, it will feel natural and right by the time you ask.

28

# Whose Responsibility To Raise Money?

Some organizations assign the job of raising money to the development or fundraising committee. Others believe it's the responsibility of the full board. Still others (large universities, arts organizations, or health providers) shift more and more of the load to staff. What is the right approach?

First, let's separate donor development from fundraising. The donor development *process* is everyone's job: staff and board and non-board volunteers. No one is excused. But, this isn't asking for money. It is developing relationships and uncovering shared values and connecting people with the organization.

There is also a core development team. These are the people for whom developing resources is a primary responsibility: CEO, board chair, development committee chair, development director, and the development committee. They are the architects and strategists of the fund raising program.

Finally, there's the board of directors. As representatives of the organization in the community, the board is instrumental in expanding the overall capacity to raise money. This ranges from the way in which the board is perceived and the confidence the community holds for it, to the role individual board members play in their various donor development and fundraising assignments.

So, who is responsible for raising the money?

When it comes specifically to *asking* for money, there is often a separation of duties. Some people just cannot, will not, or should not ask. Some have a professional "exemption" – judges usually are discouraged from soliciting even for nonprofits. Others, because of potential conflict of interest (the CEO of a similar service provider) feel they cannot ask for money. Still others just simply will not do it.

Some boards have designated askers. These are people who are moderately or completely comfortable with asking. They're willing to accompany more reluctant board members on calls and be the closers.

What is important to understand and accept in the full process of raising money – from identifying to cultivating to asking to stewarding the donor – is that the *entire board* must be involved in one way or another. It is one of your principal responsibilities.

# 29

# Your Role
# In Raising Funds

Your first responsibility in helping your organization raise funds – whatever specific role you play – is to give. Long ago we buried the excuse that "my time is money" or "I give my time so I don't have to give money."

As a board member, you've signed up to take on all of philanthropy's tasks to the degree you can – joining, serving, giving, and asking. The job is *not* multiple choice.

The late Hank Rosso, founder of The Fund Raising School and mentor to thousands of professionals and volunteers, used to say, "You can't preach religion until you get religion." He was right. If those closest to the organization aren't supporting it financially, why should anyone else?

Moreover, you have a right as a board member to be

solicited personally, usually by the chairperson and CEO. This lets you experience what it's like to be asked for a gift by a team – giving you insights into how you yourself will participate in a solicitation call.

As for your specific role in fundraising, ideally you'll play one or more of three important ones – asker, cultivator, or steward.

Asker is self-evident. You, along with team members, call on prospective donors and ask them to invest in the work of your organization.

If you're not comfortable with asking, you may want to be a relationship-builder or cultivator. Cultivators bring people into contact with the organization, listen for their interests, connect them with the people and programs that match their interests, and generally prepare them to be asked.

Lastly, stewards are there to keep the relationship going once the gift is made. It is tempting (and too common) for organizations to look at a solicitation as the high point of the transaction – forgetting that what feels like the end of a long process for the organization is, for the new or renewed donor, just the beginning of a new relationship.

As a steward, you have the great and rewarding job of keeping the donor connected.

# 30

# Serving as Steward

In the old days, asking for the gift was seen as a transaction. Plotting it on a bell curve, we built up to the solicitation through a variety of steps, first identifying the donor, then involving (or cultivating) him in myriad ways. After hitting the top of the curve – the actual moment of asking – the downhill slide began, whereby the donor was added to the file, thanked with a letter or tote bag, and on we moved to the next solicitation.

Now, we're in a different era, one of heightened competition. It is imperative today to engage donors so they will become long-term investors. And that means stewarding and deepening our relationships.

When engaging in donor stewardship, think of an "infinity loop," not a bell curve. Unlike a transaction that has to be constantly reinitiated, the momentum is continuous. Each time the loop intersects, the donor renews the gift, the commitment deepens, and raising money becomes easier, as people are already "in the loop."

As a board member, you'll need to nurture the ongoing relationship with donors (showing evidence of their gift's impact is notably important here). When you do, donors will feel invested and respond more willingly and generously to future solicitations.

You also have a role in the other kind of stewardship: stewardship of the investment itself. As a board member, you're responsible for monitoring the management and use of donor investments.

It's very difficult to raise money if what has already been given hasn't been invested well or hasn't had a high rate of "return" relative to values and impact. To ensure the proper stewardship of donors' gifts, here are three key things to keep in mind:

1) Insist on program budgets. A line-item budget is fine for reviewing and evaluating your organization's general performance, but it doesn't show how a specific program operates, whether funds invested in that program have a high or low return, and the significance of each future investment.

2) Be diligent about endowment management. The horror stories of boards that either mismanaged or unwittingly frittered away the endowment are legion.

3) Have facts at your fingertips about how money is spent. Donors will often want to know how much of their gift went for administrative and fundraising

costs, and how much went into direct services.

If your administrative and fundraising costs are out of line (more than 20 percent to 25 percent of the budget), you'd better have a good explanation. Start-up organizations can expect to spend 40 percent to 50 percent of their money for administration and fundraising, but as the organization matures and volunteers are increasingly involved in asking, that percentage should drop.

The bottom line is that there are two bottom lines in stewardship: caring for the donor so there's a solid return on values, and caring for the investment so there's maximum impact from every gift.

# WORKING WITH STAFF

# 31

# Role of the CEO

The CEO – who may be called the Executive Director, President, Director, or General Manager – has a difficult and unique role as both leader and subject relative to the board.

On the one hand, he's responsible for the day to day operations of the organization and for overseeing all personnel. On the other hand, he reports to the board who hires, evaluates, and can terminate him.

Peter Drucker calls the relationship between a nonprofit CEO and the board a "team of equals."

But sharing power is never easy. It takes clear understanding, well-defined roles, good communication practices, and mutual respect to make this delicate balance work.

The burnout rate of executive directors is unusually high. One study revealed that most executive directors wouldn't do it again. They cited these reasons: too many bosses (the whole board), unclear expectations, poor or no evaluation of performance, the board's tendency to micromanage rather than govern, lack of help with fundraising and board recruitment, and poor pay for the work required (many of the tasks of a nonprofit CEO are the same as a corporate CEO, but often for much less pay).

As a board member, you can make the role a happier one by doing your job in fundraising and board recruitment, respecting boundaries in decision-making, appreciating the work of the CEO and his staff, and by governing, not micro-managing.

32

# Relating to the CEO

Y2our relationship with the executive director depends on many variables: individual personalities, traditions within your organization, what the organization is trying to achieve, and, not the least important, your expectations.

Joe Batten, author of *Tough Minded Leadership*, tells us something most of us know: we constantly judge people based on our expectations of them. The problem is, often we don't bother to convey our expectations. We say things like, "I was really disappointed in your presentation – I expected a lot more emphasis on our programs." Of course, we never told the person what we expected.

It's the same with the balance of power between board and staff.

Find out directly what the CEO would like in her relationship with the board. In fact, have an annual session that outlines expectations. This can be eye-opening, and often it sets a tone of openness which lasts through the year.

In addition to clarifying expectations, create an environment for candor. If the CEO feels she can't bring troubling news or failures to the board, she'll stop being transparent. This can lead to unpleasant surprises.

Beyond this – and on the more personal side – keep an appropriate and professional distance from the CEO.

The reason is simple. As a board member, you may be one of those designated to evaluate the CEO. You can't let your personal relationship – whether positive or negative – get in the way of an objective evaluation.

33

# Assessing
# the CEO

The evaluation of the CEO is in many ways the board's most important function. And yet it's often neglected. It becomes a point of contention rather than a time for constructive personal and professional goal-setting.

When you join a board, ask about the evaluation policy and practice for the CEO.

• Who does the evaluation and how often?

• Does it simultaneously include a salary review or is that a separate process?

• Does the full board see the review before it becomes part of the record?

• Are there opportunities for written or verbal feedback by the full board?

• Does the CEO have the chance to respond in writing to his evaluation?

• On what is the evaluation based? Does the board as a whole see the CEO's yearly objectives or does the Executive Committee review the objectives and conduct the evaluation?

• What standardized method (or unique process) is used?

• Has the board ever sought legal counsel to ensure a proper procedure?

• Are there interim evaluations, or is the entire year brought into focus in one session?

Each year, determine with the board and the CEO what performance objectives will be used and how the evaluation will be conducted.

While no one wants to think about firing someone or having to take legal action, it can happen. Writing to the file, having interim evaluations if performance is lagging, and seeking legal or personnel advice about problematic situations are all practices of exemplary boards.

Most importantly, be objective, be fair, but be firm.

# 34

# Working with Other Staff

As a board member, it's important to stay connected to the organization's program. It is the heartbeat, the raison d'etre, the passion point that presumably drew you in the first place.

Programs are the source of inspiration, and their impact on the community is what allows you to successfully ask for money, enlist new board members, and raise visibility for the organization.

It's only natural, then, to want to have relationships with one or more staff people involved in the programs that interest you the most. But you want to keep in mind two essential points.

The first is that the people who run the programs, do the finances or marketing or fundraising, are paid employees who report either indirectly or directly to the

CEO. You are not their boss.

One of the biggest causes of burnout in nonprofits is staff people feeling that they have "too many bosses" – their own supervisor and several (or all) board members. They feel torn by requests and often get caught in the middle.

The second point is related. If staff people with whom you're working start confiding in you about the inner operations of the organization, particularly matters regarding the CEO, you must handle it carefully, openly, and in a non-conspiratorial fashion.

In some organizations CEOs forbid board members to contact program and administrative staff directly.

Know the boundaries and respect them.

## 35

# Resisting the Urge To Micro-manage

Most board members have some management experience. Better to use it to evaluate the CEO than attempt to run the organization.

Rather than govern, too many board members succumb to the temptation of micromanaging. But only in special circumstances – when there's no paid staff, or there's a true crisis – should a board be involved in management.

Instead, a board should govern, leveraging its skills through positive actions such as the following:

• Participating in the development of the strategic plan.

• Creating, with the CEO, a job description and performance objectives.

• Monitoring these objectives regularly with constructive praise and criticism.

- Attending to the regular reports the CEO provides on progress, plans, and problems in the organization.
- Employing a workable process for nipping conflict before it escalates and providing an environment in which difficult issues can be raised, not hidden.

Micro-management is time consuming, frustrating for the CEO, and ultimately nonproductive. On the other hand, good governance practices help capable CEOs flourish.

# RECRUITING AND RETAINING

# 36

# Recruiting an Effective Board

To recruit an effective board, your organization needs an institutional plan as well as a well-organized and functioning Board Development Committee.

You can't develop a plan or matrix for recruiting the types of people you need if you don't know where the organization wants to go. Planning comes first. Otherwise, recruitment will be random, and the board won't mature into the diverse, creative, far-ranging group of passionate pragmatists you require.

That said, here are a number of ways you can enhance the recruitment process.

First, respond when the Board Development Committee (see next chapter) asks for names of potential board members. You should of course be told what kinds of people are sought (expertise, gender, geography, ethnicity, race, interests).

Second, recommend, don't recruit. There are few greater setbacks to a committee that's following a procedure than to have someone announce he's enlisted a board member. While the person may turn out to be wonderful, even ideal, you need to observe the process. You owe it to the committee and to the candidate.

Third, participate in the process of getting to know potential board members. Go to a lunch, come on a tour, be willing to talk to the recruit about the organization.

Fourth, when someone is brought on the board, reach out. If your organization has a mentoring program where experienced board members are teamed with new ones, volunteer for that job. Even if there's no formal process for outreach, extend yourself anyway. Let the person know this isn't only an effective organization, it's a friendly place as well.

The last thing, of course, is to be a good board member yourself. Model the kind of action, attendance, support, humor, and enjoyment that will inspire new board members to stay around and deepen their commitment.

# 37

# The Most Important Committee

The Board Development Committee (sometimes known as the Nominating Committee, Committee on Trustees, or Committee on Directors) is the most important committee of the board.

Why? Because it determines the vitality, scope of talent, range of connections, and willingness to work of the board. And of course the quality of the board determines the future of the organization.

If yours is called a Nominating Committee, suggest the name be changed. If a committee believes it's concerned only with nominating, then it won't stay involved with the board members once they're recruited. A Board Development Committee has a much broader mandate.

The role of these four to six members includes the following:

- Preparing and implementing the policy, plan, and procedures for board recruitment.
- Encouraging board members to provide names of potential candidates and qualifying them on an on-going basis.
- Preparing and presenting a slate of board members and officers and enlisting those who have been elected.
- Organizing and conducting the board orientation.
- Continuing contact with board members, particularly those who are floundering or failing to attend meetings.
- Spearheading the board member self-evaluation and following up on the findings.

As you can see, this committee needs to meet regularly. It isn't a group that comes together several days before the nominations are due and gets on the phone to recruit a friend or neighbor to join the board.

If your organization is approaching this process in a less than thorough way, do what you can do to change that. It'll make a long-term major difference in the vibrancy and effectiveness of your organization.

# 38

# Evaluating Your Own Effectiveness

It's one thing to evaluate the CEO, but quite another to look critically yet constructively at the board and how it is functioning – as a unit, as individuals working independently, and in committees.

As with CEO evaluations, the process can feel either threatening or welcomed as an opportunity for growth. It can be randomly handled with no clear process or outcome, or it can be systematic, productive and objective.

Effective board "self-evaluations" can be done in several ways. The first is to conduct confidential interviews with all board members (the board chair and a small team of board members usually carry this out). Some of the questions might include:

- Do you still have the time, energy, and commitment to serve as a productive member?

• What benefits have you derived from being on the board? What have been your concerns or frustrations?

• How would you rate your own performance as a board member relative to your own expectations and to the performance of others? Top, middle or bottom third?

• What are your strengths and how do you feel you've used them?

• As a board member, what would you like to do, and what would you like to do better?

A second approach is to use or adapt a standard assessment tool that board members fill out. Question areas include finance, fundraising, mission, vision, and all the other board tasks.

A third way to conduct board self-evaluations is through a combination of these two approaches – filling out a questionnaire and then providing a confidential interview.

You cannot have a great board if you don't take a look at ways in which you are, can, and must work together to further the mission and vision of your organization.

# 39

# De-enlisting Board Members

Sometimes, even a once-stellar board member no longer performs well. And, too often, we let this slide for months or years. We rationalize for him – after all, he's a volunteer – and tend to make excuses long after we should.

Possibly the most challenging decision we ever make as board members is determining when and how to de-enlist one of our colleagues.

As necessary as the action might be, board members hesitate. They're concerned, rightly, about the person's feelings and how the fallout might affect the organization's reputation. What we fail to factor in, however, is that most uninvolved board members are looking for a gracious way out.

If your board chair and CEO are willing to meet annually with each board member, the angst over de-enlistment will dissipate. This is the best opportunity, in private, to ask why the person's involvement has declined.

Very often, a board member will confess she's lost interest, has an ill spouse, a new and demanding job, or other such personal and pressing matters. At that moment, the board chair and CEO can thank the person for her service, acknowledge the current situation with regret, and offer him the opportunity to step down, perhaps temporarily, until circumstances have changed.

Once in a while, a board member whose de-enlistment seemed certain will even turn things around (probably due to the special attention received).

It's important to prune deadwood on a board. But it's also key to discover why the wood is dying. Only then can you prune correctly, or water and witness new growth.

# 40

# Yearly Meetings with Individual Members

The value of a meeting with individual members isn't just for de-enlistment. While it can be a gracious platform for completing a difficult task, the majority of these intimate meetings are positive, highly praised by all participants, and a great source of board member motivation.

Chances are, your board chair and CEO have never done this. Many organizations, when introduced to the idea, ask the logical question, "Why?" They feel their board is functioning well, members are giving, and people seem pleased with their committee or task force assignments. All's well in the world.

Even if that's true, a yearly meeting with each board member will not only improve motivation, it'll also increase financial and other contributions. Why? Because board members are an organization's principal investors (even if they aren't major donors) and are deserving of at least an hour each year when they're the focus of the meeting.

Organizations which resist individual meetings cite time as the consideration. Board members won't care to spend an extra hour this way, they believe. Experience refutes this. And, if someone really resists, there's no need to press further.

Here's what is to be gained from an individual meeting. Judge for yourself whether it's worth the time:

• A confidential forum to express your concerns, desires, or issues.

• An opportunity to determine, with the organization's leadership, the nature and extent of your involvement for the coming year.

• Positive feedback for your current involvement and encouragement to stay involved in the most productive way.

• A personal solicitation of your gift that models the asking process you may be called upon to emulate one day.

In my opinion, the benefit of such a meeting can't be overstated. As a board member, it can become your annual personal renewal around the passion and purpose of the organization.

# 41

# When It's Time to Resign

Sometimes, you may wish to leave a board before your term is over. Often it'll be for one of the following reasons:

• Management has failed to respond to the board's standard for financial performance, thereby jeopardizing the organization's fiscal stability.

• The organization's mission, vision, and values have shifted or have failed to materialize as you expected.

• Other leaders on the board have either succumbed to mediocrity, ambition, or abuse of power, undermining your desire to be part of the organization.

• Your time, circumstances, health, or other conditions prevent you from fulfilling the role you agreed to perform.

• The organization is no longer your top priority, among your top three priorities, or one in which you feel your expertise can be used effectively.

Be attuned to these warning signs, and try to correct the situation if possible. If you cannot, step aside and make room for others. It is an enormous responsibility to be a board member, and an even greater one to step aside when it no longer works.

# CONCLUSION

This book began with the observation that board membership is a noble service. It is that, and more.

Being a good board member has benefits far beyond those that accrue to the organization you serve. When you invest your time, wisdom, patience, and energy to be an exemplary board member, you have a powerful impact on your community. You strengthen the capacity of the organization you serve, thereby increasing its ability to serve those whose needs your organization is meeting.

The ultimate board member is one who draws on his own gifts and talents willingly, who offers his network of contacts appropriately, who thinks beyond the boundaries when confronted with a challenge, yet thinks procedurally when the organization needs to steady its course.

As with most things, high performance is part content, part style, and part dynamics. The content of your responsibility is well defined – you have to make good decisions, raise money, champion the organization, and do the board's work.

But the style you bring is uniquely yours, and the resulting dynamic you create with others to make your board "work" is what will make the quality difference.

So, when the call for board service comes, seize the opportunity. Answer the call, spread your wings, do your best, and champion the organization. The results may resound for generations.

Copies of this and other books from the
publisher are available at discount when
purchased in quantity for boards of directors
or staff. Call 508-359-0019 or visit
www.emersonandchurch.com

Emerson
& Church
PUBLISHERS